TIGERS
A celebration of life

ANDY ROUSE

*To Carol, thanks for always putting up with
my obsessions and being the light in my life.*

*And to all those dedicated individuals, often
nameless, who work tirelessly to save the tiger.
Your work is never forgotten.*

ELECTRIC SQUIRREL PUBLISHING

CONTENTS

FOREWORD

Surely, the tiger must have been saved by now? After decades of intensive conservation effort, and untold millions of pounds, this isn't such a preposterous question.

But, sadly, the tiger is far from safe. From about 100,000 a century ago, its population has plummeted to approximately 4500 today... and counting. In fact, the situation is even worse than it seems because more than half of those survivors aren't actually breeding.

The tiger is disappearing fast.

Habitat destruction (its range has contracted by more than 40 per cent in the last decade alone), poaching (mainly for bones to be used in Traditional Chinese Medicine) and killing (to protect people and livestock) continue to take an exacting toll.

The sad fact is that there are now more tigers in captivity than there are in the wild. And this is precisely why I am delighted to recommend this magnificent book.

Andy Rouse is not a man to sit around and bemoan the plight of the tiger. He is the kind of man who tries to do something about it. The aim of his book is to raise awareness and funds for tiger conservation – indeed, a decent portion of the profits are going to conservation projects around the world.

Andy has spent many hundreds of hours in the field in many parts of Asia, working with tiger experts, to capture some of the most remarkable pictures ever taken of this increasingly endangered species. This is the spectacular result – a fitting tribute to one of the most beautiful and troubled big cats in the world.

I hope it will inspire and encourage you to support tiger conservation efforts yourself, in any way you can.

Mark Carwardine
BBC Zoologist and Conservationist

INTRODUCTION

The tiger is a worldwide and instantly recognisable icon that signifies power, good luck and courage. In the world of fashion, entertainment and education, the image of the tiger is used more than any other animal on this planet today. From an early age we learn about the tiger and we are exposed to it in different ways throughout our lives. So how could we have let such an iconic emblem of nature get to such a sorry state of affairs, where the very future of the species hangs in the balance? There are now fewer than 4500 tigers left in the wild and with each non-natural death, we are losing the fight to save the tiger. It is time to do something about this situation.

The timing of this book is no coincidence, as 2010 is a big year for tigers worldwide. It is the Chinese 'Year of the Tiger' and many conservation focused organisations, together with financial institutions like the World Bank and individual countries, are all designating a special 'Year of the Tiger'. The aim is to raise public awareness of the issues and also to provide a focus for fundraising. It is my hope that *Tigers, a Celebration of Life* will help with all these activities by showing inspirational images combined with thoughtful writing. Also by the donation of a proportion of its income from sales, it will raise some much-needed funds to help conservation work on the ground by organisations such as 21st Century Tiger.

There are six species of tiger remaining – Amur, Indian, Malayan, Indo-Chinese, Sumatran and South-China. The Amur tiger occupies two areas of the Russian Far East; one of these populations spans the border between Russia and China. The Indian tiger lives in several regions of the Indian subcontinent, including populations in Nepal. The Malayan tiger is a new kid on the block, only being named as its own species in 2004; it occupies areas of the Malay Peninsula and the southern tip of Thailand. The Indo-Chinese tiger is similar to the Malayan Tiger and is found in Thailand, Myanmar, southern China, Laos, Cambodia and Vietnam. The Sumatran tiger is the smallest of the tiger species and is only found in Sumatra. Finally, the South China tiger, which was previously found all across China, is now thought to be extinct in the wild.

That means we have only five species left in the wild and for some, time is running out at an alarming rate. It is a sobering thought that when the next Chinese 'Year of the Tiger' comes around again in 2022, we may have to modify this list down to three or even two wild tiger species left on the planet. I feel a mixture of upset and anger when I write this and just cannot believe how we have allowed this to happen to my beloved tiger.

Like most people, my love of tigers started from an early age and as a child, I always visited the local zoos to see them. You could show me all the giraffes and zebras in the world but

I always wanted to see the tigers. However, I had to wait a few more years before I actually got to work with them. When I was a student at university, I contacted the local zoo to ask for some work experience with the big cats. They agreed and for a few days I did my share of pushing wheelbarrows and cleaning out enclosures, all just to get a few minutes spent closer to a tiger. The zoo had some beautiful Amur tigers, but it was the big male in particular that fascinated me. He was so chilled out, unlike his mate who hated me with a passion, and he allowed me to watch him and observe everything that he did. I used to spend hours with him 'behind the scenes', observing how he relaxed away from the public glare. It was during this time that I managed to get my first decent animal picture of my career, which showed him drinking in his pond. It is an image that in many ways launched my career, although of course I didn't know it at the time.

On that day I made myself two promises; that I would see tigers in the wild before I was 30 and that I would one day do something that would make a difference to their survival. At the age of 24, I realised the first promise by spending several days in Ranthambhore Project Tiger reserve. I arrived full of excitement and expectation and a little bit too much belief in my own ability. Unfortunately the tigers had not been told of my visit, and all seemed to be taking a holiday over those few days, so I didn't even catch a glimpse of one. It came to the last drive on the last afternoon and after checking my meagre finances, I decided that I had to miss it. I was devastated. Just when I thought all was lost, my driver and guide took pity on me and gave me the drive for free in exchange for a few T-shirts I had brought with me from the UK.

We set off in hope and got lucky almost straight away. Without warning, a tiger strode up the bank in front of us; a magnificent wild male tiger in all his glory. He barely looked at me before walking around the jeep and along the track. It sounds like a cliché, but I sat there open-mouthed and hardly able to believe what I was seeing. I could hear the tiger breathing, smell its slightly wet fur and experience the terror that follows any contact with those piercing eyes. For the next hour we followed him, sometimes taking a different route just to get in front, so I could try to get some pictures. As a pretty awful photographer, I failed to do him any justice whatsoever and this remains the best (and only surviving) picture from that trip.

This book is perhaps the answer to my second promise, to make a difference. As a successful photographer, I know that my tiger pictures form an important tool for the conservationist, but I have always wanted to do more. It was Sarah Christie, the Zoological Society of London's tiger expert, who first told me about the significance of 2010. An idea began to dawn and after a few brief phone calls, *Tigers, a Celebration of Life* was born. Self-publishing your own book is a major undertaking that usually takes months; this book was written and completed in two weeks. I have packed it with all my best tiger images, real-life experiences and some interesting facts that you may not know. I have also included a detailed conservation section which has information written by leading experts on the current status of the tiger and what is being done to arrest its decline.

This book really has something for everyone, and it is my hope that it will, at the very least, raise some funds for tiger conservation projects in the field. I also hope that children will be encouraged to read this book or attend one of our special 'tiger talks' for 2010. Children are very much the key to the future of the tiger as they will become the next generation of decision makers, and will have to continue the fight long after the current generation have gone.

So can we save the tiger? From my perspective, it represents the ultimate test of the will of humankind to save a species from extinction. If we don't save the tiger with all this effort, then what hope is there for any other species? 2010 is the time for all of us to make a stand, to ensure that the tiger does not become a museum exhibit of the future. It really is up to us, as the tiger is just an innocent bystander and like us, it has every right to be on this planet.

ONE AMAZING DAY

We all have amazing days in our lives; those that stand out from the humdrum and stick in our memory forever.

In my life as a wildlife photographer, it has to be said that I have had some pretty amazing days, but perhaps none more memorable than one incredible 12-hour period in Ranthambhore Project Tiger Reserve. I was there one April, at a time when my favourite tigress Machali and her three 18-month old cubs were about to go their separate ways.

The morning dawned bright and clear and we found Machali early on in the drive, thanks to some langur alarms. These ever-watchful monkeys tell everyone when a tiger is close by and their haunting calls led us to the right place. Machali appeared, walking slowly through the forest towards us. We were inside the only jeep present so were able to set up well ahead of her path. I took this image through the trees which was a bit of a challenge, but I thought it made a nice habitat shot and something a little different.

We followed Machali for an hour or so; clearly she was on a mission as she continued in a dead straight line. Finally she led us right up to one of her cubs, that was relaxing just off the track. It was not unusual to find them apart, as, over the past weeks, it had become increasingly difficult to get pictures of them together. With low moans they greeted each other briefly before playing in front of us for some time.

Abruptly Machali ended the play, walked off and headed for some bushes. 'There is another cub there,' whispered Dicky, my friend and guide. She disappeared behind the bushes and, almost immediately, we heard the sounds of a fight. The noise was incredible! We edged slowly back and forth along the road, trying to get some kind of view. Unfortunately the fight was right behind the bush and the shot opposite was all I could get. Check out those claws – this was no play fight! After a few seconds, the fight was over and with a lot of growling and deathly looks, the cub sidled off into the undergrowth. Nothing much else happened during the morning and we left Machali sleeping, with no sign of any cubs anywhere.

In the afternoon, we found Machali again a couple of kilometres away, but this time we witnessed a much closer fight completely in the open. The cub managed to land a pretty good left hook before Machali's size and sheer power took over and the cub quickly retreated.

We followed Machali down the track, thinking that she might drink at the river, and we parked and waited. After a few minutes, Saleem (my driver) pointed behind us; a cub had appeared on the track and was making a beeline for Machali with a very determined look on her face.

As she drew level, we could see a porcupine quill buried in her neck. Young tigers will often tackle porcupines. I guess everyone has to learn that painful lesson once, but it could not have helped the cub's mood at all.

The cub passed by us, broke into a run and jumped straight on Machali. She was clearly taken by surprise and for a second, I thought that the cub was getting the upper hand. Then, all hell broke loose as the mother of all fights started between them.

Annoyingly, I had a tree right in the way of my shot so I had a choice: to move and get a better shot but risk disturbing them, or stay and hope that they moved. It was an easy decision and I stayed put as any ethical wildlife photographer would. Wildlife always takes precedence over photography. It was also the right choice in terms of getting the shot, as they soon moved onto the road.

The ferocity of the fight caused the hairs on my neck to stand on end and the noise was absolutely terrifying.

Machali had her claws out and raked them several times over the cub's body; once again, her power won over and the cub limped off. We just sat back staring at each other, hardly daring to believe what we had just seen. It had been such an amazing day, as we had witnessed behaviour that was so difficult and unusual to see in the wild, let alone photograph.

The image you see here was awarded Highly Commended in the 2009 Veolia Environment Wildlife Photographer of the Year awards, which made me very proud. Awards aside though, I will never forget the noise of that big fight.

CLOSE UP

A tiger's face has true beauty and shows hidden stories of life.

By now, you will have gathered that there is one tigress that has a very special place in my heart. She is big, very beautiful and can look damn mean when she wants to! Many portrait photographers have a muse (a model that they love to photograph) and mine is Machali, which means 'Lady of the Lake.' Born in the monsoon of 1997, she has occupied the core area of Ranthambhore National Park since then, raising four litters and never being fazed by her army of admirers. In 2009, she was awarded the Lifetime Achievement award from the Travel Operators for tigers organisation, as they estimated that she had contributed $10 million per annum to the local economy. She is one special big cat.

Yes, it's her again! Getting great tiger portraits is addictive and the secret is pretty easy. First you need to have a beautiful subject; all tigers are certainly that. Then you need low or overcast 'diffuse' light. This is to ensure that the eyes are fully open and that shadows from the eye ridges do not cause the eyes to have 'half moons' across them. Finally, you have to ensure that your shooting position is below eye level, which can be a challenge when you are in a jeep – but who said photography was easy? But that is not quite the final bit ...you should always keep a smile on your face, as you are photographing one of the most beautiful animals on the planet.

··· If India had a king and queen of tigers, then Machali would be the queen and this guy would be the king. He is called B2, lives in Bandhavgarh National Park and yes, he is huge! I have rarely photographed him, but on this occasion, I came across him licking his wounds after a major fight with a territorial rival named Bokha. Male tigers defend their territory with passion and you can see from the fresh wounds that it must have been a very serious fight indeed.

··· Here is the previously mentioned Bokha, arch-rival to B2 and seen here a few days after the fight. Looks huge as well, doesn't he? Well, for an Indian tiger he is, but compared to the male Amur tiger you see here (···), he is pretty small. Of course, the main noticeable difference is the amount of extra fur on the Amur, since it has to endure the coldest conditions of all the tiger family with temperatures in its environment (the Far East of Russia) plummeting to -40°C.

Tigers have a highly-developed sense of smell, but sometimes they need that little bit of extra sensitivity. This is usually needed to read the information left by other tigers (and other animals) in the form of scent marks. At the back of their mouth, they have the highly sensitive vomeronasal organ, whose purpose is to decode information from scents.

To get the scent to pass across the organ, tigers draw both lips back, which naturally draws the scent to the back of the mouth (I know you are all trying to do this yourself now!). This is called the flehmen response and a lot of mammals use it to determine all kinds of information from a scent mark. Two days before I took these shots, I had witnessed a tiger scent-marking this very tree. Clearly it had left a calling card and this tiger would be able to determine the sex of the tiger that left it, its oestrus state (if a female of course) and how long ago it was left.

Tigers are very expressive and communicate either by scent-marking, facial expression or vocalisation. Their calls range from low moans to full-on snarls and their visual communication can be equally as expressive.

In the image above, the tiger is showing 90% aggression and 10% fear, as this shot was taken when the tiger saw another one approaching in the distance. If this tiger was attacking and being really aggressive, then as well as the flattening of the ears you see here, the edges of the mouth would also be curled up, revealing the canines.

Ever wondered what those spots are on the back of a tiger's ears? Well, we will probably never know for sure, but there are a few popular theories. The first is that they are a defensive mechanism for cubs against predators, as the spots look like the eyes of a much larger predator when viewed from behind. Another theory is that the mother uses the spots to silently communicate with the cubs in situations when any vocalisation may be dangerous; when the cubs see the spots they know everything is cool, but when the mother puts her ears down, they know that danger might be close by, so they stay still. However, perhaps the most plausible theory is that they are a sign of aggression and that when tigers pull their ears slightly back (which effectively rotates the white spots to face forward) it gives a warning to others not to approach.

Certainly, the third theory might hold the most water and, in my limited practical experience, I have seen this happen several times. The image opposite was shot when another tiger approached and both white spots were instantly in view. If you check out the tiger fighting pictures in this book, you will see that some of the shots show that the white spots are clearly facing forwards, towards the other tiger.

‹••• Of all its senses, a tiger's hearing is the most developed and the one it depends on the most. It uses its hearing to detect the sound of prey running through leaves or across the forest. I have seen a tiger suddenly stop walking and listen, and not long after that, heard deer running through water. After a few more seconds, I saw it move off in the direction of the noise and disappeared into the forest where I could not follow. Research indicates that tigers can differentiate between different prey just by sound alone, which helps them make the decision whether to go and investigate or not. Their hunting prowess is much more highly developed than many people imagine.

•†• Since tigers depend on their teeth for chewing tough prey, they cannot afford to be without any during the growing process. So the adult teeth grow behind the milk teeth and push them out – a process which ensures that they always have a full set. This Indian tiger, photographed in Ranthambhore, is exposing its teeth during a yawn, clearly showing the development of the huge upper canines. This one is relatively young and still has a way to go before its canines are full-size.

•†• The older a tiger gets, the more it is prone to losing teeth. You can see here a snarl from Machali, revealing the tremendous cost of her fights shown earlier in this book. Losing so many teeth will make killing prey and eating it more difficult. As I write this today, it has been a year since these shots were taken and she is still alive and well. Clearly tigers can adapt to almost anything – as long as we leave them alone.

HUNTING

Watching, stalking, waiting, charging…killing.

The tiger is a fearsome predator but faces several challenges in order to achieve a successful hunt. The first challenge is that the tiger is dealing with a prey species (generally deer) that has a highly developed sense of self-preservation and is always alert. The second is that this prey species can be spread over a vast area. The third is that unscrupulous tourists may interrupt a hunt. I have seen this many times and have always been careful to stay in one place and not alert the prey to the tiger's presence. After all, we are just visitors to the tiger's realm and it is living a real life. So this collection of images is my homage to the tiger's hunting prowess.

The home range of a tiger varies according to the tiger species, as there will be different densities of prey in that specific habitat. Also, being a big cat, no tiger will ever travel farther than is necessary in order to get food. In general, Amur tigers have a much harder time finding food than their cousins. Their main prey – wild pigs and deer – are spread far and wide and therefore Amur tigers often have to travel some distance for their food. Fortunately, the tiger is a very adaptable predator and Amur tigers will eat almost anything that they can catch, no matter how small. They need to adopt this strategy because a male Amur tiger is the heaviest tiger species on the planet and, living in such cold climates, they use up a lot of energy and never quite know when they will have their next meal.

A tiger's stripes gives it the ultimate camouflage pattern. They serve to break up its outline in dense vegetation and the grasslands in which it hunts; you might think that the exception is the Amur tiger, but it too is a forest dweller. The stripes are unique to each tiger and also differ between different tiger species, but all allow the tiger to blend into its surroundings. This image shows an Indian tiger that I photographed in a dense area of forest. Although we could hear alarm calls, we could not see it until it moved slightly; this was proof that the camouflage really works.

Tigers spend a lot of time watching and observing prey. I guess that they must be calculating their chance of success and the best route for an ambush. Like all predators, they are also looking for any weaknesses in their prey which they can turn to their advantage. This Indian tiger was watching a group of chital drinking at a waterhole and he stayed in this position for several minutes before deciding that an ambush was impossible and dozing in the sun was a much better option!

🐾 Looking at this image, you might wonder why the sambar are not running away. The answer is simply because they know they are completely safe, as the tiger is not an endurance runner and relies on stealth and camouflage to get close to its prey. If they can see the tiger, then it presents no danger to them as they can easily run away. You might also notice that the sambar on the left has its tail raised and is walking away. The underside of the tail has a pattern that equates to a 'follow me' signal that others can see, to alert them in times of danger.

Tigers can stalk in almost any habitat. This is the incredible tigress Machali, patiently stalking across some very open ground towards a herd of deer. I remember thinking she was so obviously visible that surely the deer must see her. However, every movement she made was deliberate, taking each step with painstaking care, before putting her paws silently down. Every muscle in her body was tense and her eyes were always focused straight ahead. Tigers are incredibly patient hunters; she took over 20 minutes to cover 10 metres of ground and only the alarm of a distant langur stopped her being successful.

In forest and jungle habitats, tigers are supreme hunters. We watched as the cub shown here stalked a chital stag for over an hour. It patiently followed the stag, always keeping its scent downwind, never rushing and never losing patience. Several times we thought that it was about to charge, but each time, the stag moved just at the wrong time. Then, when the stag came out to feed on a track, the tiger crept out and waited. It pulled its legs underneath its body so that it could charge at a moment's notice. Both my friend Dicky and I thought that it was a dead cert and had every camera imaginable ready for the charge. We kept absolutely silent throughout, not wanting to cause the deer to become scared by us and move away. The silence was deafening and as the stag slowly made its way across the road and into the forest, the tiger just stood up and stretched. At that point, the stag saw it and ran off barking, but at no time in the previous hour did it have a clue that the tiger was so close. Tiger hunts are like this – a real game of cat and mouse – and you can never second guess what the tiger is thinking... or when it is going to charge!

* Tigers are similar to lions in their hunting strategy. Like lions, they are only able to run fast over very short distances, so they use their amazing camouflage stripes and the natural terrain to get close to their prey before that final charge. They need to get within 20 metres (ideally 10 metres) and be at full speed before detection, in order for the hunt to have any chance of success. It is said that they can reach a maximum of 35 mph (55 kph) during this time. Only 1 in 20 hunts are successful and of the 50 or so hunts I have seen, I have only witnessed a kill a handful of times – and only photographed one once.

* Tigers are incredibly powerful animals and, as you can see here, they have highly-developed forelimbs which they use to grapple their prey. They need all of this power as they regularly tackle deer species that are several times their own body weight. In the 1980's, Ranthambhore had its own crocodile killer, as one tiger was known to have killed several crocodiles. Truly, the tiger is an amazing powerhouse.

It is rare to witness a hunt from start to finish, but on the last day and very last drive of my most recent trip, I witnessed a very special one. The hunt took over an hour from beginning to end, and the young tiger must have stalked for over a kilometre through the grass before the final charge. Just look at the focus on that face; those incredible eyes are already surveying the prey (a group of chital) for any signs of weakness or injury. Every step was calculated and made with a purpose.

After stalking downhill, the tiger used our jeep as cover to cross an open road without being seen. If we had moved it would have alerted the deer, so we just sat still and enjoyed this magnificent predator being so close. The tiger then continued its painstaking approach; in the background, you can see the deer is oblivious to what is happening. It is incredible to me that the tiger would even consider covering this open ground, but it did, and slowly got within range of the unsuspecting deer.

The deer started moving away and as soon as all their backs were turned, the tiger charged at full speed. I tracked it through the camera as it hit the first chital and knocked it straight up into the air. Instead of being knocked down, it fell onto its feet and made a quick escape as you can see here. That day, it was the luckiest deer on this planet and the tiger knew that it had missed its one chance. Just to sit and witness life and death always humbles me and makes me realise that we have such easy lives in our modern society. Perhaps if more of us saw the tiger and its struggle for life, then the species would not be in such dire straits.

Of course, sometimes even the most experienced tiger can mess up a hunt. Here is supreme hunter Machali, yes, the one we saw stalking a few pages ago. Well, some time after that shot was taken, she managed to get right up to the sambar but could not see it over the hill. It was a comical situation, as the sambar could not see the tiger and the tiger could not see the deer; a bit of a conundrum for both! All confusion ended when a pair of watching eyes from a distant hillside issued a warning bark and the deer wasted no time in taking the hint.

❧ Tigers eat a wide variety of prey and rather than putting in the usual shot of deer, I thought that I would show something different. The prey here is a honey badger. I am not sure if the tiger actually caught it, as we only came across her on the first drive of the day, but if she did, then she deserves a special predator medal. The honey badger is a fearsome animal and I have seen it take prey from a fully grown leopard. However, tigers are great opportunists and if the chance was there, I am sure that this one took it without hesitation.

❧ Tigers are unquestionably beautiful, but so is their prey. The elegant chital from India is an incredibly graceful animal, but also a fast runner when it needs to be. So, on this page you will see a celebration of the beautiful chital. Remember that they too are suffering a decline in numbers due to poaching and habitat reduction. In fact, it is as vital to conserve them as it is to conserve tigers, so they deserve a place here and our respect.

LIFESTYLE

A big cat's world.

Tigers have a very varied lifestyle from the day that they are born until their last breath. In this collection of images, I wanted to show some different aspects of their behaviour, from the way they raise their cubs to their absolute fixation with water. Of course, like all big cats, they like to relax and sleep a lot too...

Tigers spend a lot of time walking and their home territories can vary from 50 to 1000 square kilometres. This may seem like a huge range, but the governing factor is the number of prey in the area. Tigers will do the least amount of work possible in every aspect of their life; if they live in a good prey area, they will not need to walk far. Conversely, the Amur tiger generally lives in areas where the prey is spaced over a wide area, so they have to walk much farther.

This beautiful female is approximately four to five years old and is one of Machali's daughters. She is called Bachhi and walking quietly through the forest, she is not in a hurry for anyone.

The home range of a tiger bounds many others. In places where they intersect, tigers leave calling cards in the form of scent marks. Tigers can get a lot of information from these scent marks; in fact, it is one way that a male tiger can find a female who is ready (and willing) to mate.

Late one afternoon, we came across an Indian tiger scent marking all along a track. Initially, it would sniff a prominent tree and often show us the flehmen response as it drew the scent across its vomeronasal organ. Then it would turn round and spray the tree with its own scent mark, clearly leaving its own message.

Tigers are obsessed with water, which is so unusual for a big cat (with the exception of the jaguar of course). As the year progresses and the temperature increases, they become more bound to water and during the oppressive summer months are rarely out of it.

This is a rare shot of an Indo-Chinese tiger in water. They live in remote areas of Thailand, Myanmar, Vietnam, Cambodia, Laos and Southern China. Not much is known of this tiger as it has been rarely studied, but it is estimated that the population numbers are fewer than 1200 as it has suffered heavily from poaching. Tigers usually only immerse their back end in the water and rarely immerse their whole bodies. However, they will swim if necessary and will spend many hours in the water during the heat of the day.

This serene image was taken early one morning as a young male Indian tiger walked across a dam. This male tiger, which we nicknamed 'Flame' due to the markings on his side, had most of his territory outside the Bandhavgarh National Park. The part inside the park included the lakes. Unfortunately, the two local dominant males, B2 and Bokha, share it too.

The first we knew of this tiger was a sudden alarm call from a chital herd. A minute later, the grassland was empty; the next minute, there was a tiger striding confidently across it. I began to get excited when I realised it was going to walk straight across the dam. It was a shot that I had been wanting for several weeks without any sniff of success. The reflection when he crossed was simply amazing and to see such a young male, unscarred by life and in such a beautiful place, is an image that will stay in my mind forever.

There are not many young animals that can match the tiger cub for the 'cute factor'. Tigers make great mothers and are incredibly protective of their young, staying with them for at least 18 months. These images are a work-in-progress, as I have never been lucky enough to work with a mother and young cubs for an extended period of time. However, the lure of spending time with tigers is never one that quite goes away and I am sure that I will get lucky one day – perhaps for the next book.

Female tigers are in oestrus several times a year and during this time may spend two or three days mating with the territorial male. The gestation period for a tiger is 103 days and after that time, the cubs are born blind and usually in litters of two or three. They are tiny at birth, weighing only 2-3 pounds, and their eyes only open after 7-9 days. They rely entirely on their mother's milk for several months until they are weaned.

A tigress will have a large home range. Within this area there will be several places where she can safely leave her young cubs while she hunts. On this occasion, we found the cubs inside a cave and were careful not to approach too close. Cubs are very inquisitive and we did not want to encourage them to leave the safety of their cave.

Cubs have many predators when left alone; leopards will kill them if they get the chance and infanticide from unrelated male tigers is not uncommon. Research indicates that through predation or the results of human action, less than 50% of cubs reach maturity and independence.

Early one morning in Bandhavgarh, we found this six-month-old cub hidden in some undergrowth by the road. The mother was hunting nearby and the cub knew to stay still and quiet, as the mother might not get a second chance.

My first experience on elephant back at Bandhavgarh was with this female and her two cubs. It takes a long while to get used to working from an elephant, as they are liable to shift at a moment's notice. Luckily, I was with Kuttapan, the king of all mahouts. He skilfully took the elephant up through a rock gully (we had an off-road elephant) and there in front of us were two almost fully-grown cubs.

The female slept a short distance away, her belly full after a good hunt. At this age, the cubs are starting to get independent and soon will begin to compete with their mother for food, which results in only one outcome. Check out the 'One Amazing Day' group of images to see what I mean.

At 18 months old, some cubs become fully independent. This is one of Machali's, fully-grown and out by herself after all the fights. Although she still looks like a young tiger, I watched this one hunt successfully several times; she obviously had a good teacher. So, another generation of tigers reaches maturity and with it, hope for the future of these amazing cats.

Tigers are very active in the mornings, particularly during the hottest months of the Indian summer. For the tiger photographers who endure the heat for the love of their art, this time of the day is certainly much valued as well! After a lovely drive down into the park on a perfect morning, we were all alone in the queue for the park. There, just a few minutes inside was this lone tigress, just chilling out in the sun and clearly enjoying the cool morning air. I love this image as it really shows the habitat of Ranthambhore and the tiger completely at home within it.

Ranthambhore is full of ruined palaces and temples, which add a beautiful visual dimension to the park. One of my obsessions there is to photograph the resident tigers using every single one of them; so far I have about 90% and counting. This ruined palace is right at the entrance to the park and I wish that I personally had found that lovely shady spot, as the temperature was 45°C!

This is another image showing a tiger using one of the ruins in Ranthambhore. This time, the tigress was using the height of the temple to look straight into the forest. Just look at those beautiful back stripes, so rarely seen. We watched her for several minutes until she stealthily crept down and stalked off slowly. A few minutes later, a herd of terrified chital erupted in a burst of calling from the forest. One of their kind would call no more after that day.

This is the grandest view in Ranthambhore, with the queen in residence. Machali looks out over her domain from the cool spot of this old palace. When I look at this image, I am so glad that I included the whole of the temple rather than zooming in closer. This is one of my favourite tiger shots from Ranthambhore; a vision of calm and tranquillity. This location was totally different to the place from which I shot the image, as I was among a number of jeeps, all competing for the best position to see the queen.

CLOSE ENCOUNTER

I have been in many dangerous situations in my career, but perhaps none sends shivers down my spine more than the day I was stalked by a wild tiger…

Despite all their power and hunting prowess, tigers have only ever scared me on one occasion. Only once have I ever felt hunted and had those eyes lock onto me, in a way which was more than just out of curiosity.

It started off as a normal morning and we found Machali down by the lake. She was keeping off the tracks, making any photography quite difficult. She did give me one shot, the image you see opposite, with the ruined palace in the background, but I got the impression that this morning we weren't going to see much of her.

Any Machali sighting always attracts a lot of jeeps and this morning we had the full complement. However, the great thing about Ranthambhore is that the jeep numbers are always limited, so it is never really an issue. Saleem, my expert driver, was always in front. That was good, as he could give Machali plenty of space and stop other jeeps trying to cut in front and push her away. Eventually she disappeared into the forest where we could not follow, and the jeeps all started to disappear to look for other things.

However, Saleem and Dicky both knew Machali well and decided to try a big detour to the other side of the lakes. There was a small chance that she might be heading to that location, where there would be no other jeeps. We switched off the engine and waited patiently for about two hours, straining every part of our hearing for any tell-tale sign of a tiger.

As we were starting to give up, she appeared out of nowhere and walked straight at the jeep.

I shot from the lowest angle possible and she fixed on me with a straight stare. Knowing Machali well, I wasn't scared of her and a second later, she had looked beyond us like we didn't exist. She quickly disappeared into the forest again; all was quiet and we wondered where the cubs were. We would soon find out.

We left the park and started our way back to the Ranthambhore Bagh, which is Dicky's hotel and permanently open bar. Along the access road, we hit a traffic jam and after a few minutes, we were told that there were lots of vehicles stopped ahead of us because there was a tiger at the temple! We edged closer and from our position, we could just see the temple ahead of us. It was actually the burial site of a Muslim holy man. The green cloth that you see is used to cover his grave as part of a religious ceremony. Take a close look at it...

Yes, it's a tiger! One of Machali's cubs had walked out of the national park and into the boundary zone. It had obviously decided to explore the temple and seemed fascinated by the burning incense. After staying on the vehicle for a few minutes, Dicky and I decided to go on foot and join the rest of the crowd watching the tiger. I made the mistake of only taking my big lens.

The scene was incredible. A sea of local tourists were holding up their camera phones to get a picture of the tiger; meanwhile it just stood at the end of the temple watching the free show. I wish I had taken a wide-angle lens to show the crowd with the tiger in the background.

I was not comfortable being there and neither was Dicky, as the tiger's ears were already showing signs of threat. The Forestry Department turned up then and started marshalling everyone away as they could see the potential danger of the situation. We decided to head quickly back to the jeep. It was farther back down the road and we had to walk back around the corner. As we reached the apex of the bend, both Dicky and I stopped at the same time, as our peripheral vision told us something was wrong. There, right on the track was a second tiger and it was walking straight towards us.

The eyes were fixed right on us and although I knew that we should be leaving, the wildlife photographer in me made me stay just a few seconds longer – just long enough to get a shot that I will never forget.

The tiger started to look at us more intently and you can see here the head coming down slightly in this shot. That was a signal for us to leave and we went very quickly back to the jeep, which we then had to reverse up the road. The tiger emerged from the forest seconds later, gave us a long lingering look and then disappeared into the forest on the other side of the road. I have thought about this encounter many times in hindsight. The large crowd had gathered at the temple because most locals never get to see a tiger in the wild and this was an incredible privilege for them. Of course, it was extremely dangerous and I can understand why the Forest Department were going frantic when they found everyone just standing there. However, it is also a good thing for locals to see a tiger as they will have a lifelong memory of it and attribute a value to it. The more locals (and especially children) that see tigers, then the better it will be for the future of the species; only by seeing it in real life can you truly appreciate how special the tiger is.

GETTING GREAT PHOTOS

*Many of you reading this book will be photographers
and hopefully the images that I have shown so far will
have inspired you to shoot some pictures of your own.*

A professional insight. In my opinion, tigers are one of the most beautiful animals on the planet to photograph. To get a stunning picture of a tiger is a wonderful achievement, but they are actually surprisingly difficult to photograph. Perhaps it is the emotion of seeing them so close, either in the wild or in captivity, but ALL of us get over-excited and just snap away, forgetting the basics of photography!

When you are building up your tiger image collection, try to take a variety of pictures to tell the story of a tiger's life. Taking only portraits may give you some beautiful pictures, but your portfolio will have little variation. So these following pages will hopefully help you to combat this problem with some well-chosen tips that come from my years of experience. You will also notice that I have not mentioned gear in this section. That will come in the following 'Travel' section of the book as I always consider the artistic side of photography to be far more important than equipment details.

As photographers, we all have a role to play in tiger conservation. Whether we are photographing in the wild or in captivity, we have a responsibility to the tiger to photograph it well. When you show pictures of a tiger to friends, family or members of your local camera club, you are acting as an ambassador for the tiger. If you show a beautiful picture then people will remember it and will want to find out more about the tiger. The more people we have in the tiger fan club then the better chance we will have of saving it for future generations to love too.

Purrfect portraits. The tiger is such a beautiful cat that the classic portrait is usually everyone's most desired picture. The trick with a great portrait is to keep the background simple and try to get the main focus point near to the eyes. You do not need to have eye contact; sometimes this makes a picture too threatening. In the image opposite, the gentle feeling comes directly as a result of the diffuse (almost pastel) background and the tiger looking past the camera. I used a Nikon 200-400mm lens. This is the only zoom lens I would use for portraiture, as my normal choice would be a fixed focal length lens. The latter gives much better facial compression than a zoom, with the exception of my beloved 200-400mm! In this case I set the aperture at f/8 to get good depth of field on the face and manually selected the focus point between the eyes. Of course f/8 will also bring some background into focus and distract from the tiger, so when you're shooting try to use a 300mm lens (or larger) and sit further back. If you need to use a zoom then use it at the maximum range rather than getting too close. In this image the light was very diffuse, which helped the eyes shine clearly and did not over-expose the highlights; in bright sunlight white areas can be overexposed but generally following the meter on the evaluative setting will yield decent results.

A walking tiger. Tigers spend a lot of time walking and for most people it's all the tiger action they are ever likely to see. Machali obliged me on this occasion with this lovely walking shot. The most difficult thing about it was the timing, as she kept flicking her tail out of the frame. Tigers are quite slow and deliberate when they move, so you do not need a very fast shutter speed to freeze the motion. About 1/250sec should counter their movement and the excitable shaking of the photographer. Do try to keep the focus point squarely on the bridge between the eyes during the motion as this will give the sharpest-looking result. The aperture in this case can be as wide as you like, as much as f/2.8 if you wish, as you are only worried about the front of the tiger being in focus. A zoom will be much more useful than a fixed focus lens here as you can keep the tiger in the frame until it is right on top of you. For this shot I used a 70-200mm f/2.8 with a 1.4x teleconverter.

Using tracking focus. Once in a lifetime you may get the chance to photograph a charging or running tiger. If you can hold your nerve and keep your adrenaline from spoiling the shot, there are a few simple things that you can do to ensure it is sharp. The first is to use the aperture priority setting and set the widest aperture of the lens, say f/4, which will by default select the fastest shutter speed possible. The second is to set the ISO to 1000 or more; it is better to get a sharp shot with a little noise than one that is technically perfect but blurred! The third,

and perhaps most important, is to set your camera's autofocus to servo / continuous / tracking mode so that the focus changes with the tiger's position. If the tiger is running fast at you then you will need to give the autofocus several seconds to work out the speed of the tiger. Don't panic and just keep your shutter button pressed halfway until you can see it lock. Firing continuously may sound good but often it misses the moment, as the autofocus system doesn't have time to work. Be calm, pick your shots and they will come.

Artistic tigers. There is always a place in my photography for abstracts as they show another dimension to an image collection. Here are three examples, all shot in the wild.

The two main images show a more 'artistic' view of a tiger running. For obvious reasons this type of shot only works when the tiger is running across the frame. To take them, simply use a shutter speed around 1/15sec and pan the camera to match the motion of the tiger. The faster you pan the more streaky lines you will get, but also the more indistinct the tiger will become. I think that for these pictures to work well, the head of the tiger has to be pretty recognisable. Everything else can be a blur and the image will still work. I love this kind of picture and one day I will publish a pure 'art' book on big cats. Many amateur photographers are reluctant to try shooting this kind of image and I think it stems from a lack of confidence. However, if you do not try and do not continually challenge yourself, then your photography cannot improve.

Using the zoom blur technique created the image on the right. For this shot I braced the camera securely, set the shutter speed to approx 1/15sec, and turned the zoom ring sharply while taking the shot. This technique only works if you zoom back from the subject and hold the camera very securely as you cannot afford any motion at all. It is a hit and miss technique and will probably require quite a few goes before you're successful. Luckily for me on this occasion, the tiger wasn't going anywhere.

So go on, try a few artistic images. You never know, you might actually like them.

Habitats. Tigers live in beautiful habitats and if you are photographing them in the wild, it seems to me a real crime not to include the habitat in any shots you take. This is Flame, my favourite young male from Bandhavgarh. I took a few images with the lens zoomed right in, then noticed the reflection of the tree in the water and decided that it made a really beautiful natural frame to the tiger. If you rush your photography and blast away with the motordrive, you miss all of these subtleties; take your time, take a few shots, then take the camera away from your face and look with just your eyes. In my opinion it actually takes more skill to take a landscape-style shot that works rather than a straight portrait, something I mentioned in my previous book *Living Landscapes.* As for camera settings I used an aperture of f/8 for this image, to give it some depth.

Including landmarks. India has some amazing forts and several tiger reserves have fine examples of them. Perhaps the easiest to photograph is the imposing one that dominates Ranthambore; a fort has stood on the site since 944 AD and countless generations of tigers have walked underneath it. These days the image that you see above is a common one to shoot. Unfortunately I have only managed it in really harsh light. I used a circular polarising filter here to give the sky and water some colour. Note that the focus point is on the tiger as I manually selected the focusing point; do not use the automatic setting, as it will focus on the fort! An aperture of f/8 is sufficient to get everything pretty sharp with a wide-angle lens, and for this shot I used a 24-70mm.

Abstract portraits. Following on from the previous pages on abstract images, there is no reason why you can't apply a little art to your portraits as well. My thought behind the image above was to create something that would capture the essence of a tiger without showing the whole of the tiger, to just give an impression of the face and the body. I also wanted to use the moody light that I had for once and this seemed the best way to do it. Of course, the head needs to be the point of focus. That means manually selecting the focus point again, which needs to be done accurately in the heat of the moment. I chose a very wide aperture here, f/4, as I wanted only the head in focus, and used the shallow depth of field to give a suggestion of the stripes behind.

The 'tiger in habitat' approach can also get the abstract treatment too. Often, when I find tigers, they are in deep undergrowth and I have watched many photographers just give up and move onto something 'easier'. In my experience there is always a way to see the face or eyes of a tiger clearly. All you have to do is to look though the viewfinder and move around a little. I used this technique here together with an off-centre composition to make the picture a little more interesting. There are no set rules for composition; everything in photography is personal choice so don't be afraid to take pictures that you like, no matter what others might think. One person's art is another's nightmare.

Zoo tigers. Not all of us are lucky enough to photograph tigers in the wild and there has always been a short-sighted attitude from some photographers about images of tigers in zoos and animal parks. Later in this book you will find a very eloquent piece on the role of tigers in captivity from Sarah Christie, the Zoological Society of London's tiger expert. There is nothing wrong with photographing tigers in captivity; that is where I first started and initially discovered my love of tigers. For most photographers this is the only option that they have. This is also sometimes the only way of getting images of the more elusive tiger species. The above images

were shot with the help of my friend Tim Redford. They show an Indo-Chinese tiger and were photographed in captivity, as a wild shot would have been impossible.

I think that getting a great picture of a captive tiger can sometimes be more difficult than in the wild. First you have the bars to contend with, and trying to get a naturalistic-looking picture in some enclosures I have seen is a challenge at best. The issue with bars is a commonly misunderstood one, as some photographers maintain that you can zoom through bars and make them disappear. What actually happens is that the bars are blurred due to the shallow depth of field, but they are still

there and you can still see them. The worst thing is that sometimes they cover the tiger's face, thus making it appear slightly out of focus.

Of course there is not much you can do about this in some zoos, as the enclosures are designed for the benefit of the cats and to keep the public safe. But increasingly, zoos are providing enclosures with glass panels or with open viewing areas where you can look into the enclosure (usually from a high point or across a moat) and these areas can be great for photography. My suggestion for you is to find out the location of these areas in your local zoo and arrive when the zoo opens. This is vital as

the cats will be more active and the light will be good. It's the same for the end of the day. Finding out when the cats are fed is also vital. This will happen on just a couple of days during the week and it is best to avoid the day after feeding as all you will see is a sleeping cat!

Some zoos and private collections are now offering special 'cat photography' days and these are by far the best option for the photographer. They give you all the access that you need while under the watchful eye of highly-trained staff.

SAVING THE TIGER

If you were not a tiger fan before you started reading this book, you should be one by now. I hope you're willing to help us in the fight to save the tiger from extinction. Believe me, it is a fight that we can win.

So, this final section of the book will look at the threats to the tiger, what is being done to address them and what you can do to help. I will also use some of my experience to help you plan the ultimate trip to see and experience tigers in the wild. As part of the research for this book, I wanted to find out what tigers really meant to people. Therefore I asked my Twitter followers, plus those who regularly read my blog, how they felt about them. Here's a selection of their responses:

'We must act urgently so that we can say that we are the generation that DID something to save them, NOT the generation which made them extinct.'

'To me, there is beauty in all things touched by Mother Nature, but is there anything more beautiful than the tiger?'

'Having a wild tiger stare you full in the face is like going back 30,000 years in a single leap.'

'The ultimate example of power, elegance and fragility.'

'The most majestic of big cats. It mustn't be allowed to become extinct because of greed, fear or ignorance!'

'Magnificent, elegant, majestic, proud – all things to be treasured, not lost.'

'We don't have the right to deny this species its existence, or future generations the chance of enjoying these magnificent creatures.'

'Don't let a book be the only way to see this magnificent creature in the future.'

'Tigers embody everything that is wild, beautiful and dangerous about the world we live in; the world would be infinitely less exciting without tigers in it.'

'To me, tigers represent a goal: to one day show my son and daughter these beautiful animals in the wild and help them appreciate their unique majesty. I can't do that if they're extinct.'

'Tigers were made by God, and loved by humans. They should always be around for our children's children's children to enjoy.'

'If, during my lifetime, I get to see a tiger living wild and free, I will consider it a life well-lived.'

'Coming face-to-face with this majestic creature sets every nerve tingling, your senses are on maximum alert and you realise "you are just like him." His spirit is your spirit – but his fate is in your (man's) hands. How can we not preserve this awesome species?'

'Because beauty is spelt in five letters. T, I, G, E, R.'

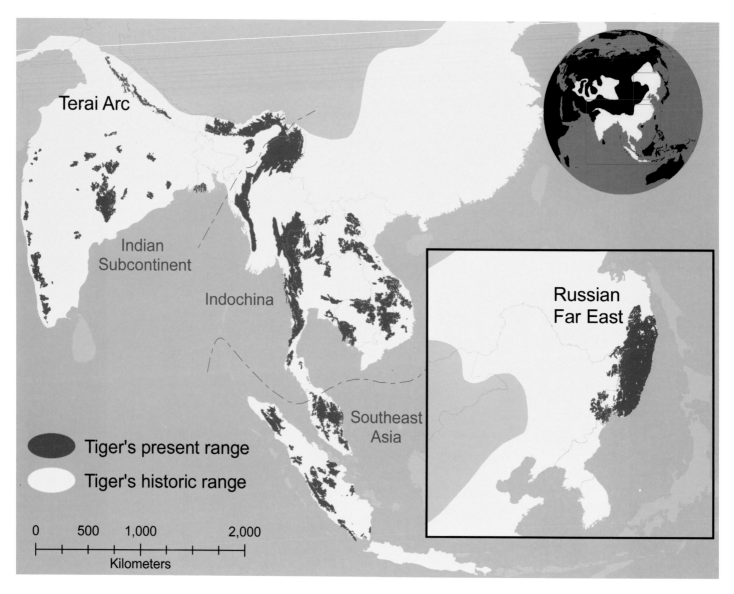

THE CURRENT SITUATION

Sarah Christie is the tiger conservation expert at the Zoological Society of London and 21st Century Tiger. I asked her to write about the current status of tiger populations and talk about her views on how the tiger can be saved. Her response makes compelling reading.

SAVE THE TIGER, SAVE THE PLANET?

Sarah Christie
Zoological Society, London

People feel strongly about tigers. Those of us who have come face-to-face with a living one never fail to be moved, whether we are urban dwellers uplifted by the sheer beauty and power of the beast – seen safely from elephant-back or inches away through glass in a zoo – or rural villagers experiencing rather different emotions following an unprotected encounter on foot in the forest or a dawn raid on their cattle. From Hindu gods and Indonesian spirits through to national emblems and sporting mascots to Tigger of Winnie the Pooh fame, this magnificent cat has occupied a key position in the human psyche for millennia. It is the world's favourite animal, as shown by an internet poll of 74 countries in 2004. Even in areas where people live next door to tigers and risk losing livestock or even friends and family to them, it is possible to find passionate advocates for their conservation.

Clearly, however, strong feelings are not enough for us to ensure that tigers will still walk the jungles of Asia and the forests of the Russian Far East in the 22nd century. Tigers are hard to count, and only recently have accurate estimates become available in at least some parts of their range. This means that although we can estimate that we have somewhere between 3-5,000 wild tigers left today, we cannot put a number on how many there were 50 or 100 years ago. However, we don't need an accurate graph of decline to know that tigers, along with most other wild creatures and virtually all the wild places left on earth, are fast losing ground.

Tigers are not only losing their forest homes to the inexorable march of human population growth and economic development, they are also threatened by deliberate killing for the illegal trade in wildlife parts, by competition with humans for their preferred foods – deer and pig, which humans also kill both for food and for sport – and by retaliatory killings when (perhaps driven to it by loss of natural prey) they take cattle or goats from local farmers. The interests of the tigers and the people appear diametrically opposed, and it is not surprising that most range state governments can muster little political will to tackle the problem, nor funds to train and equip forest protection staff.

Tigers need large areas of undisturbed forest, whether we are talking about the home range of a single tiger or the space needed to maintain a viable population over time. Over the last few decades, the forests of Asia have shrunk and fragmented at a rate which has implications far beyond the survival of a single species, however iconic. As Asia's economies gather speed, soon to overtake the western world, forests are consumed by large-scale industrial agriculture and mining operations. The rate of loss is alarming to say the least; in Indonesia alone, an area the size of Wales disappears every year.

However, in a way, it is this very situation that may offer us a last chance to save wild tigers. It is becoming clear that humans need forests too, and not just in terms of the luxury of being able to visit them for pleasure, or of income for local residents through harvesting products like rattan, bamboo, fish, fungi or honey, to name but a few. No, humans need forests to hold our planet together – to maintain an environment fit for life. Forests maintain watersheds so that rivers can continue to flow all year round, and they prevent topsoil from being washed away in heavy rain. Most importantly of all, they produce oxygen and sequester carbon dioxide. Stopping the destruction of forests in Asia, as elsewhere, is a key part of any global strategy for the long-term well-being of the human race.

And forests need their animals – the flora and fauna within them are parts of an interdependent whole and tigers, being at the top of the food chain, are good indicators of overall forest health. To support a tiger population, the forest must be large and it must be full of tiger food. Deer and pig are top of the menu, but wild cattle, monkeys, smaller mammals and even fish, reptiles and birds can also figure in a tiger's diet. Tigers also make great 'flagships' for conservation, whether the focus is on ecosystem services such as carbon, or on individual protected areas for their own sake. Tigers rarely fail to generate interest in the media and the public alike, and they provide stunning images. Making tigers symbolic of efforts to stop deforestation in Asia provides us with an instant emotional connection and a way to engage widespread public support. Also, as we approach the Chinese Year of the Tiger in 2010, we also approach a chance to tie tiger survival to global survival via international carbon trading agreements, a chance we should not miss.

We are all getting used to being asked to offset our carbon footprint by purchasing carbon credits, for example when we fly. Given the choice, would we rather buy a faceless carbon credit generated by planting a timber crop on degraded land, or a 'tiger-friendly carbon credit' produced by stopping the illegal destruction of a national park? A tiger-friendly carbon credit that would not only protect all the other animals in the park, but also safeguard the livelihoods of the local residents who rely on the forests for their own income? Easy question, really, isn't it? It's a win-win situation; the tigers and other wildlife would gain, the local people would gain, the planet's carbon balance would gain and the carbon trading income from the park would turn it, in the eyes of national and local government, from a financial drain on their resources to a key income generator well worth looking after.

There are few other options with the potential to make forests full of tigers and other wildlife worth money to the governments and people who have to live with them – worth more money than they would be chopped down. Ecotourism can work well in areas with high tiger densities and relatively open terrain such as India and Nepal, but carbon trading offers a real opportunity for countries where this is not possible. It is a first step in getting industries to pay for the real environmental costs of their activities. Other options for 'offsetting' our impacts on the environment are also possible, and once living forests are generating income, political will to protect them will not be far behind.

Of course, just saving the forest will not help tigers in the long run if they continue to be killed individually. Their recent disappearance from some of India's famous Tiger reserves has been reported around the world, and in Southeast

Asia too, there are parks and forests where deer and pigs still live, but the tigers are mostly gone. This is primarily due to the illegal trade in wildlife parts, which stimulates poaching all over tiger range. Just like illegal drugs, many wildlife parts are high in value in proportion to their volume – ivory, for example – and so attract criminals.

The key items in the trade in tiger parts are skins and bones. Tiger skins periodically come into fashion as rugs or wall hangings, most recently among the emerging middle classes in nations like Russia and China. Sadly, they are often popular among high-ranking officials from the military, police and government – the very people whose job it should be to stop the trade. The powdered bones are used in traditional Chinese medicine (TCM) to cure ailments such as rheumatism and arthritis. Other parts of the tiger such as eyeballs, whiskers and even the penis are also used, but while the media like to highlight these grisly items, the bones are worth far more money to the traders.

So are we once again coming up against a conflict between the needs of people and the needs of tigers here? In saving the tiger, might we be depriving people in many parts of Asia of important remedies and damaging their cultural traditions? The answer, I am pleased to say, is no. For the major item, the bones, none of the ailments addressed are life-threatening and there are other remedies in the TCM medicine cupboard that have similar effects, while the other items belong in folklore rather than in modern TCM. The various associations of TCM practitioners in China, and elsewhere around the world, have all declared that they do not need and will no longer use tiger parts of any kind in their medicines. These are responsible, professional people, and they have no desire to drive the tiger to extinction or to be perceived as doing so in the eyes of the world.

So, tiger bones have been removed from the officially approved list of remedies in China and their sale is now entirely within the black market. However, there is still one group attempting to promote their use, for reasons of self-interest. A few rich businessmen in China who own 'tiger farms' have for some years been trying to promote the ludicrous idea that allowing them to make enormous amounts of money from battery farming of tigers, and a consequent production line of legal tiger bone medicines, would flood the market and stop all poaching of tigers in the wild.

The arguments against this idea are almost too obvious to mention; illegal products would be much cheaper to produce, there would be no way of telling legal products from illegal ones, wild tiger parts would always command a premium price in the eyes of the consumer and, given the size of the population of China, the level of demand that would be produced by legalisation of domestic trade could never be met by battery farms.

As it is, even within the illegal trade, the vast majority of medicines labelled tiger do not contain any tiger bone, because there is simply not enough to go round. Leopard, lion, and even dog and goat bones are used instead. The government of China, which should be congratulated for long ago declaring domestic trade in tiger parts illegal, must decide how to handle this internal pressure. Awareness and information programmes aiming to reach both the politicians and the consumers are therefore vital and celebrities like Jackie Chan, among others, have taken the message to the Chinese media.

So, it seems that the two major strands of action that are needed to ensure wild tigers will still walk the earth when our children's children are old, are just about within our reach. The first is a realistic global mechanism for funding the survival of forests with wildlife living in them; the second is a continued effort to stop the demand for tiger parts, both skins and bones. Alongside these, there are many other important steps to take. Increased international and national investment in law enforcement is essential to prevent international wildlife trade on the one hand and local trade and poaching on the other. Measures to ensure that those who must live alongside tigers are compensated for any livestock losses and protected from harm themselves are also crucial, along with careful separation of infrastructure development activities like dams, roads and mines from key forest areas. Voluntary, properly handled resettlement of villages from within protected areas is another win-win situation where money is available. It provides the villages with better services and housing, the wildlife with undisturbed habitat, and the country in question with intact ecosystem services.

All these things and more must be done. But the key issue, at the heart of it all, is to make forests full of tigers and other wildlife worth more standing up, living and breathing, than they are

going up in smoke or on the backs of timber lorries. Save the tiger, and save the planet too? Can we? Well we can give it our best shot. If we don't, when the next Chinese Year of the Tiger rolls around in 2022 it may be too late. And if we as a species cannot protect wild tigers with all their symbolic meaning, the most potent icon of wildness that we have, if the last wild tiger dies in a poacher's snare, a corner will have been turned, a light will have gone out in the world and in our hearts. Saving the tiger is a test. If we pass, we get to keep the planet.

Sarah Christie

THE ROLE OF TIGERS IN ZOOS

As you will have read in the Introduction to this book, my love of tigers comes from working with them in a zoo environment. Even today, some people still hold the outdated view that zoos have no place in conservation. I completely disagree. A tiger is a tiger, whether wild or captive and most people would never see one, or learn to care about them, were it not for zoos. To back up this point I again asked Sarah Christie, tiger conservation expert at the Zoological Society of London (ZSL operates two zoos as well as conservation projects in over 40 countries), for her views on the role of zoos in tiger conservation. Here's her reply:

'We should consider captive populations of tigers as the PR agents for their wild cousins. Modern zoos and wildlife collections make vital contributions to conservation and their main function has moved well beyond the traditional view that they are there only for our viewing pleasure. Most visitors usually overlook these contributions, as they are often hidden, so here are a few of the most compelling arguments for zoos playing a role in conservation of tigers and other species:

1. A healthy gene pool for the future – this is often thought of as the primary reason for zoo conservation breeding programmes, to maintain a gene pool for possible future re-introduction to the wild. But the primary goal of zoo breeding programs is to help to generate enough support for the species in the wild to make sure reintroduction is never needed. In general, reintroduction is difficult, time consuming and expensive, and even more so when it involves large carnivores capable of killing our domestic livestock or even us. It is *not* impossible – young captive tigers could easily learn to hunt without help from their mothers if given the chance – just like your domestic cat did – and we could even teach them to be scared of humans (just as important as knowing how to hunt)

– but circumstances in which it is the right thing to do are very thin on the ground indeed, especially for tigers. Reintroduction should only ever be undertaken if there is no possibility of natural regeneration of a wild population, or of translocation of wild animals from another area, and only if all the causes of decline have been dealt with. So whilst zoos are of course conserving a managed gene pool of tigers suitable for reintroduction if it is ever needed, reintroduction by itself is not the goal. There are other, less obvious but certainly equally important ways in which captive tigers help save their wild cousins – and zoos are managing their populations to stay healthy over many future decades in order to contribute via all these channels, not just via the potential for reintroduction.

2. Awareness, inspiration, education – whatever name you prefer to use, there is no doubt that zoo tigers are vital ambassadors for their wild relations. There is no substitute for seeing one in the flesh and feeling that pang of fear as it looks you straight in the eyes. Many significant tiger conservationists work, or have worked in the past, in zoos. The author of this book, Andy Rouse, has already said that his love of tigers came from seeing them in zoos at an early age. Seeing tigers in the wild is great of course, but for the vast majority of people reading this book it will remain just a dream. In contrast, zoo tigers can reach a wide cross-section of society, because zoo audiences are not limited to those who are already passionately interested in wildlife and because many zoo visitors are children. Children are the future of conservation and a great experience of a tiger at an early age will carry through into adult life; the child may grow up into someone who can make a difference. Thus, instilling an interest in

conservation of wildlife in people from all walks of life while they are young is one vital role zoos can play.

3. Fundraisers – zoos can also use the interest their tigers generate among visitors and the media to actively support tiger conservation in the field. For example, 21st Century Tiger and ZSL channel a great deal of money raised from zoos – mostly in the European and Australasian breeding programmes — to the field. Add to this the efforts of other zoos which have their own tiger funding programmes, such as Minnesota in the US and Dreamworld Zoo and Steve Irwin's Wildlife Warriors in Australia, and we find that over 10% of the annual NGO (not government) budget for tiger-focused conservation between 1998 and 2005 came from the world's zoos, or through them in the form of grants. For Sumatran tigers, which have long been a focus for all the above-mentioned zoos, the figure is even higher at over 50%! This is an incredible figure and clearly shows the real benefit of zoos in tiger conservation.

4. Finally, there are lots of ways that zoo tigers can help in terms of information and training. For example teaching wildlife vets how to use anaesthetics, and contributing blood and faecal samples for genetic research. And let's not forget the pictures! Great images like those that you see in this book are vital for conservation as they reinforce the message in a more accessible form.'

Sarah Christie has provided us with some important insights here and you can see that we both feel that zoos have a vital role in conservation. Specifically, they make a telling difference to tiger conservation and will do so increasingly as we enter the difficult years ahead. So the next time you visit a zoo, spend time looking at their tigers and think to yourself what it would be like in 30 years if they were the only ones left in the world. Hopefully it will make you want to act, to do something to make a difference. Don't think that just as one person you cannot make a difference. After all, just one person wrote this book; any contribution to the future of tigers is a telling one, no matter how small. The following pages will give you some ideas.

MAKING A DIFFERENCE

By now the tiger fan in you will be raging and wanting to do something to arrest the decline of this amazing cat. At first glance this seems like an impossible task, because much that needs to be done is at a governmental and enforcement level. This is true to an extent, but support from the grass roots upwards can make a huge contribution if you channel your enthusiasm in the correct way. I will give you a very simple example.

I have a conservation fund with Paramo Directional Clothing, called the Aspira Fund, where we donate all of our profits from a branded clothing range to small and often ignored conservation projects worldwide. When I was working in Ranthambhore I became aware of a project to stop the tigers straying from the park while looking for water. In the summer months the tigers that live on the fringes of the park have no water and their only alternative is to go outside the park and drink water from village waterholes. This brings them into conflict with local people and livestock, with potentially catastrophic results for both.

To help tackle this problem, local conservationist Aditya Singh worked with the National Park to identify where bore holes could be drilled to bring water to the surface. He located several places and with the help of local contractors, and funding from local hotels, he dug a series of new waterholes. Our Aspira Fund paid for one of them – not an earth-shattering amount, just a few thousand pounds. We also paid for the guards to be there initially and I am pleased to report that the first night we flooded the waterhole, a male tiger came to drink. That is what I call conservation in action.

So why did I tell you that story? Simply because I am a nobody, just a normal guy who loves tigers, but, by raising funds through clothing sales, I helped make a difference and may have saved a life or two ...each life is vital. Here are some suggestions on how you can do the same:

See wild tigers. Support tiger tourism by saving your pennies and seeing these wonderful cats in the wild. See the following section for more details.

Support zoos. Go to your local zoo and see the tigers, see what fundraising activities they are doing and get involved. Take your friends to the zoo and most importantly, take children and show them tigers.

Education. Today's children will inherit the fight for the tiger and we must get them involved at an early age. Teach your own children about tigers, make it fun and involve face painting and role play. Then take it one step further and go into your children's school to involve them too.

Boycott tiger products. We need to ensure tigers are worth more alive than dead. If you are in Asia and are offered medicines that purport to contain tiger bones / body parts, do not buy them. You may think buying these products stops others from doing so, but you are actually supporting the illegal trade.

Vote with your wallet. Whenever you can, if you're buying products made from wood, make sure they're from sustainable forests. In the near future it should become easier to buy palm oil from companies that are at least making an effort to ensure their plantations don't do too much damage. To call them 'sustainable' may be pushing it, but let's say they're more sustainable than the rest.

Support NGO's. There are many Non-Governmental Organisations that focus on tiger conservation and other related issues. They do not receive any government funding for their work and are entirely dependant on public donations for their daily operations. Of course, there are many organisations competing for your donations so check out their websites carefully and see where your money goes. Make sure that 100% goes on conservation projects in the field; if in doubt, write and ask and then specifically ask for your donation to be spent on a tiger project. Check to see if the projects have a scientific or educational slant too, as persuading local people to conserve the tiger is vitally important.

If you are offsetting your carbon footprint in the future, look for projects that support the existing habitat rather than replanting new habitat (preferably in tiger range); these should become available soon, and we need to preserve the balance within the ecosystems that we have now, not new ones for the future. Also see if the funded projects are run from afar, or by locals. As I've said before, having local involvement is vital to the success of any project. I am not going to recommend a long list of organisations here as there are many great people working for the conservation of tigers that I do not know about. But the organisations listed here are amongst the ones that will be supported from this book.

21st Century Tiger. Since its inception, 21st Century Tiger has raised over £1.4 million to fund more than a hundred carefully-chosen conservation projects in eight Asian countries. The projects cover a wide spectrum of requirements for tiger conservation. They include scientific research and monitoring, education programmes, training for wildlife rangers, support for anti-poaching units, uncovering networks of illegal trading and advice in cases of human-tiger conflict. 21st Century Tiger gives 100% of all donations received to these projects and is a unique fundraising partnership between the Zoological Society of London and Global Tiger Patrol. Website: www.21stcenturytiger.org

Freeland Foundation. This is an international environmental and human rights organisation that works throughout Asia, raising public awareness and political will. Based in Thailand, Freeland concentrates on awareness activities and providing direct training and technical assistance to police, customs and environmental agencies to combat poaching, illegal logging and human trafficking. It recently ran a very successful awareness campaign, via leaflets and posters at customs houses, border crossings and airports, to stop people buying and keeping wildlife as a pet (which includes tigers). Website: www.freeland.org

Panthera. This is an NGO that specialises in the conservation of the world's cat species. By working through partnerships with local and international NGO's, scientific institutions, and local and national government agencies, Panthera has brought together passion, expertise, and large-scale strategic thinking. Currently Panthera has two main tiger projects, Tigers Forever and Tiger Corridor. Website: www.panthera.org

The Environmental Investigation Agency. The EIA is an independent campaigning and intelligence-gathering organisation that fights wildlife crime. It often goes where others fear to tread and has a great reputation for success, although it is rarely mentioned in the media. The EIA has several very important tiger initiatives, all of which focus on the critically important area of reducing the demand for tiger products and making them worth more alive than dead. Website: www.eia-international.org

The Phoenix Fund. This Russian-based conservation organisation focuses entirely on the endangered wildlife of the Russian Far East and specifically the Amur tiger. It has several excellent projects, including anti-poaching, education and also compensation schemes for livestock loss. Website: www.phoenix.vl.ru

The author and Aditya Singh in front of the Ranthambhore water pump as it started to fill the new waterhole. This was paid for by the Aspira Fund, as mentioned opposite.

RESPONSIBLE ECOTOURISM
Living the dream, seeing wild tigers

One of the best ways to support tiger conservation is to go and see them in the wild, as you will be helping to make them worth more alive than dead. Tiger tourism has its issues, but it still remains a great way to get money into the local economy and show the worth of tourism. Currently only India and Nepal have tourist-friendly tigers and they reap the benefits. In these states, tiger conservation and tourism go hand in hand. In the other range states we have to look at other ways to help the tiger (such as the carbon trading previously mentioned). So in this section you will get the benefit of my travel experience to help you plan your perfect trip. It could be you in one of these jeeps living the dream.

To give a local insight to the benefits of tiger tourism I asked my friend, Ranthambhore hotelier and local conservationist Aditya Singh, what it all meant to him.

'Wild tigers in India have tremendous importance,' he said. 'Tigers are the apex predators and their survival is crucial for the preservation of wild habitats, which in turn is crucial for India's water security, as most of our rivers originate in tiger reserves. Besides, tigers have crucial socio-cultural and religious value for most Indians. They are India's best-known brand ambassadors and are an important part of Hindu religion.

'Tiger tourism is incredibly important to India as it is often the only economic industry around the reserves and has a vested interest in saving the reserves. It is estimated that tiger tourism contributes nearly a billion dollars to the Indian economy every year and a large part of this sum goes to the most poor and neglected parts of India.

'I own and run a small 46-bedded lodge called The Ranthambhore Bagh, on the outskirts of Ranthambhore National Park. We provide direct employment to about 40 local people, including our staff and indirect employment to over 200 suppliers, drivers and guides. All of them are from the small towns and villages nearby. Before we trained them to deal with tourists, almost all of them were making a living by illegally exploiting the resources of the tiger reserves. They now make a decent living through tourism and realise the importance of wild tigers. In other words they turned from the tiger's enemy to its biggest supporter.

'If, for some reason, tourism would die out in Ranthambhore, then these same people would have no choice but to go back to their old ways. Unfortunately for India, our conservationists and decision-makers, who are often far removed from the ground realities, choose to ignore the conservation value of tiger tourism. It is high time in India that we realised these important benefits and started using tiger tourism as the most potent conservation tool that is at our disposal.'

Photo reproduced courtesy of Aditya Singh

A TOURIST'S VIEW

So you have seen the benefit from a hotelier's point of view, but what do the tourists themselves think? I asked three of my clients, who have all recently accompanied me to India, what the experience meant to them.

Darren Clark, Middlesbrough

'I can vividly remember the day when I saw my first wild tiger. My wake-up call was well before the sun had cleared the horizon and we headed off in the jeep with a cloud of dust trailing behind us. We searched the jungle high and low while looking for the elusive cat, but to no avail. The only signs of its existence were the pug marks left in the dirt of the road.

'In the afternoon we traded the jeep for the 4x4 of the jungle, an elephant. We searched in all the well-known hiding spots; it was brilliant fun but still no tiger. Then we climbed up the side of a huge rocky outcrop to a small cave at the top. In the cool shadows of the cave we saw one of biggest tigers in the park. It was such a moving experience and I felt so privileged to view such a sight. He watched us closely out of the corner of his eye as we approached to within mere feet of where he lay and then dozed away peacefully.

'To see one of the few remaining tigers in the wild was the experience of a lifetime. I realise what a privilege it was to see such awesome animals in the wild and it really brought home to me that we really must protect the tiger. It would be such a tragedy if future generations could not share in such an incredible experience.'

Darren Clark

Steve and Alison Rogala-Kaluski

Steve and Alison Rogala-Kaluski, London

'From time to time opportunities arise in your life, which you have to seize when you get the chance. Being able to travel to India to photograph tigers was one of those moments. Even though we had seen countless images and natural world documentaries about tigers, nothing prepared us for that first encounter. Whether you see a tiger from a jeep or from the back of an elephant, its size, weight, posture and sheer power and assertiveness is one you can never forget. It was also refreshing to see the local guides just as excited as we were to see a tiger; they were delighted and proud to share those moments with us. The highlight of the trip was to see a tigress immerse herself into a small pool of water and lap vigorously to quench her insatiable thirst, whilst gazing straight into our eyes. It was an awesome moment that neither of us will ever forget.'

Clinton Lewin, London

'I remember the first time I saw a tiger in Ranthambhore. It strolled majestically across the track and gave me a long lingering look, as it came to within ten feet of us. I didn't know whether to shoot pictures, video or just to watch; in the end I did all three! Within a few minutes, the tiger disappeared into the forest and my first encounter was over; but the memories though will stay with me for a lifetime. Tigers are simply beautiful and to get up close and personal with them was just so exhilarating and the realisation of a lifelong ambition. I even produced a calendar to sell in Clinton Cards that, I'm glad to say, sold well and raised money for 21st Century Tiger to help conserve this truly wonderful big cat. I would recommend anybody who's thinking about going, to stop thinking about it and just go.'

Clinton Lewin

TOURISM NOTES

I hope by now that you feel truly inspired to plan a trip to see tigers in the wild in either India or Nepal. The first thing you need to know about going to either country is that nothing is rushed and life can be relaxingly or frustratingly slow, depending on your point of view. You must allow plenty of time to visit the reserves. Just turning up for two days and expecting wonderful tiger sightings will lead to disappointment. Instead, plan your itinerary with extra time to allow for delays and don't just concentrate on tigers. Both countries have a wonderfully rich culture that is an incredible assault on the senses, so take the opportunity to enjoy this aspect too.

Where to go. There are many tiger reserves in India and Nepal and if I were to detail all of them it would fill up another book. So here, in my opinion, are the top few reserves for visiting on your first tiger-watching trip. Spending enough time at these reserves will guarantee you some sightings that you will never forget.

Chitwan and Bardia, Nepal. Most tiger sightings from these parks are from elephant back (see below) and both have the added attraction of the highly endangered one-horned rhino. Tigers can be elusive due to the habitat and long grass, but the scenery is beautiful and there is plenty of other wildlife to keep you entertained while you are waiting for those stripes to appear.

Ranthambhore, India. World-famous Ranthambhore's tiger populations were decimated by poaching in the 90's but are now in resurgence and offer great opportunities for tiger photography. The habitat is a mixture of dry forest and desert scrub, with plenty of open areas. There are also a number of lakes and the ruins of old palaces, which give the park a very special feel. This is the home of my beloved Machali and about 80% of the images in this book were taken in Ranthambhore. This is my favourite tiger reserve and if the sightings are good here there is no better place; it does

pay though to check ahead and see what the sightings have been like. Routes are strictly controlled with only 5 jeeps and 5 canters per route; a canter is a specially designed low-level open bus, for the budget minded tourist. There are plenty of accommodation options but I recommend staying with Aditya and Poonam Singh at the Ranthambhore Bagh; they can arrange everything that you need and Aditya is a great photographer too. Website: www.ranthambhorebagh.com.

Bandhavgarh, India. Perhaps the most visited tiger reserve in India, Bandhavgarh is situated in beautiful teak forest and is dominated by an imposing fort. There is a large population of tigers here. Safari is by jeep only, routes are strictly controlled in the mornings and afternoons to keep the number of jeeps on a sighting to a minimum. Bandhavgarh is the place to see tigers if you want to go for quantity in the shortest possible time; most of the lake shots in this book are taken at Bandhavgarh. Again there are many places to stay but I always stay with Rhea and Shalin Ramji from Junglemantra. They offer great hospitality, are conservation-minded and know what tourists want. Website: www.junglemantra.com

These are the main parks that offer the best chance of seeing tigers, although please do not forget parks such as Pench, Kanha and Corbett as they also have tigers, plus many other reasons to go there. I do suggest though that if this is your first trip that you stick to either Bandhavgarh or Ranthambhore and then visit the other parks when you have some good sightings in the bag. Visiting other parks is essential for tiger tourism to work as a conservation tool, as all local economies have to benefit, not just the chosen few.

When to go. The tiger season roughly runs from early November to mid-June. Before this period is monsoon season and afterwards the heat is unbearable unless you are a camel (and a tough one at that). If you visit early in the season, say November / December,

then the mornings will be brutally cold and the daytime temperature very pleasant. For a photographer the light is simply the best at this time; everywhere will be beautiful and green, although this can make the tigers hard to see. As the season progresses it heats up and daytime temperatures can reach 50°C by June. Tiger activity can increase with the hot weather, as they have to make frequent trips to water. However, the downside is that they can be active only for very short periods of the day. Nevertheless, this is my preferred time of the year. As a good compromise, choose February, which has better light than June and less vegetation than November – but you may still need your jumper in the morning!

What to take. The most important thing is a smile – that is always appreciated. Take the minimum of clothes, especially if you are travelling by train; laundry is dirt cheap anyway. Don't be fooled into thinking that India is always hot as the mornings can be very cool, and you should take something warm. For those of you who suffer from stomach issues, some travellers have found using non-dairy acidophilus tablets helpful. They provide good bacteria that will fight the naughty stuff that wants you to spend your trip on the toilet.

Camera gear. It's always difficult to offer advice on gear. Personally, on my last trip I used all of my Nikon equipment – from a 14-24mm lens to my beloved 200-400mm. For the best all round shots you will need to use lenses up to 400mm in focal length and I would always use a zoom for flexibility. Perhaps the best combination for the average tourist is a 70-200mm with a 1.4x converter on a camera with a cropped sensor. Of course, a bigger lens will get you much closer; if you have a 500mm then take it, but it will only be useful in a jeep (see below). Don't forget to also take a wide-angle lens as the habitats can be beautiful and tigers will come close. I always use a high-end compact camera for these pictures as it is small and always with me. A tripod is next to useless unless you have your own vehicle. Instead take a beanbag and fill it at the hotel with rice or chickpeas.

Elephant rides. If you are going to Bandhavgarh then some of your tiger-viewing will be from elephant back. This is great fun as you will move through the jungle at a relaxing pace and at a height where you have a great view all around you. My first tip is to take the minimum kit with you and certainly not any big lenses or tripods; a 70-200mm zoom is usually good enough. There are two reasons. The first is that the elephant is an unstable platform and has the habit of continually moving when you are trying to take your picture. The second is that you'll need both hands to fend off vegetation that is trying to remove your head from your shoulders and you won't be able to worry about protecting an expensive lens. I'd definitely advise that you take an old pair of gardening gloves with you for the elephant ride, otherwise your hands can get ripped to pieces. Saying all of this, I recommend that you should take the opportunity of an elephant ride whenever it is offered, as it's a lot of fun.

Ethical behaviour. I have seen some really horrid behaviour from tourists at tiger sightings. This has included people standing up, screaming, shouting, arguing with tourists in other vehicles and being verbally abusive to guides. No wonder tigers are sometimes scared of jeeps. Sometimes I am scared of jeeps too. Instead of the calm atmosphere normally associated with wildlife, a tiger sighting can be complete chaos. I sometimes feel ashamed of the behaviour I witness and I have occasionally left some tiger sightings to find my own peace elsewhere; I am just disgusted by what I've seen. We are ambassadors for our own culture. How can we expect local cultures to behave differently towards tigers if we do not?

So when you go out on your tiger safari, please behave with respect to everyone. If you feel that your driver / guide is pushing too close to the tiger then tell him to stop, as you are paying him and in control. I am very lucky as I work with incredibly ethical drivers and guides, but that only comes with experience. Just remember you are on holiday and to see a tiger is a privilege and not a right.

Local Cultures. Responsible tiger tourism can only help save the tiger in India and Nepal if it benefits the local community. There are many ways in which you can make this difference; here are just a few suggestions.

1. Try to stay somewhere that provides assistance to the local community – you can see what I mean from Aditya Singh's comments earlier in this chapter. Travel Operators for Tigers uses a pugmark ratings system for accommodation according to its contribution to responsible tourism. Use this as a guide and not a bible as some lodges are not included that should be. For example, Junglemantra in Bandhavgarh does a lot of community outreach work but is not included in TOFT. The hotels that operate responsible tourism are generally not the usual big-name chains but the small family-owned ones. Try these for your stay instead, as you will get a genuine, warm and friendly welcome and a lot of extras that you would never get anywhere else. If in doubt, write to them and ask what they do for the local community. Some hotels bring in their own workers from other parts of the country and this does not help responsible tourism!

2. Ensure that you spend your money in the local community and not in the overpriced hotel gift shop. When in Ranthambhore I always visit the local women's collective, where local villagers are employed making clothes for tourists. Buy gifts from stores in the street, buy ice creams from a roadside vendor; every little thing makes a difference.

3. When you tip, make sure that you tip the people that count. That includes your driver and guide of course, but also the hotel staff that helped you – they are all locals. But don't tip the hotel manager – he is paid a lot more than the staff!

So now you've reached the end of the book. When you put it down, please don't forget about the tiger until the next book comes along. 2010 (the Chinese Year of the Tiger) gives us all a unique opportunity to help, a chance to all work together and stop the decline. I am not so naïve that I think it will happen overnight. However, if enough of us want to save the tiger then we will. The power is entirely with us.

I understand how some of you will wonder why you should bother, as the tiger's environment is far distant from your own. I can understand how the daily worries of family and work life will take priority over one big cat's struggle for survival. But this fight for the tiger represents so much more than it first seems.

The tiger is the ultimate wildlife celebrity of our society, a symbol of the power and feeling of nature. Our efforts to save it from extinction are the ultimate test of our will to protect the planet's wildlife; if we cannot save the tiger, what hope is there for any other species?

It is my sincere belief that WHEN we save the tiger, it will signal a change in how we look at wildlife and will inspire us to save many other endangered species. It will send a message from generation to generation about what can be achieved and hopefully we will never let this talismanic species be brought to the edge of extinction again. So let's end this book on a positive note: we CAN save the tiger, we HAVE to save the tiger and we WILL save the tiger.

My sincere thanks to the following special people:

Sarah Christie, Mark Carwardine, Aditya and Poonam Singh, Rhea and Shalin Ramji, Saleem Ali, Mr. R.S. Shekhawat , Kuttappan and his sons Joseph and Raju, Tim Redford, Ellis Dor, David Clark, Lee Crawley, Jeremy Gilbert, Colin McCarthy, Andrew Jackson, Keith Fielding, Carol Tang, Charlie Sammut, Troy Hyde, Tim Harris, Anup Shah (for the inspiration), Martin Carter, Darren Clark, Steve & Alison Rogala-Kaluski, Clinton Lewin and all who have travelled and shared my tiger adventures.

Special thanks to mentor and designer Eddie Ephraums, who worked incredibly hard to get this book ready in a fraction of the usual time. Thanks Ed for turning a passionate idea into a reality.

First published in Great Britain 2010 by Electric Squirrel Publishing Studio 10, Apex House, Trethomas, Glamorgan, CF83 8DP, UK. www.andyrouse.co.uk

A catalogue record for this book is available from the British Library.

ISBN 978-0-9564575-0-9

Design and production by Eddie Ephraums www.envisagebooks.com

Printed and bound by CandC Offset Printing, China

Picture declaration: Images in this book have had basic colour correction, but no additional manipulation. A few pictures were taken in controlled conditions. They have been included as they show behaviour that would otherwise be impossible to illustrate. The vast majority of images, however, were taken completely in the wild and are a testament to patience, extreme luck, a reluctance to never give up and a love of all things striped!